Just a little girl in a 34 year olds body!

Laeshia Vance

BookLeaf
Publishing

India | USA | UK

Presentation by *BookLeaf Publishing*

Web: www.bookleafpub.com

E-mail: info@bookleafpub.com

ISBN: 9789363300293

First edition 2024

ACKNOWLEDGEMENT

There are things in life that happens and it feels so bad. And yet, there are things that feel so good that you feel like wow, this has to be the best feeling. Then that feeling is beat with another best until you realize, wow. LIFE is always a prize. Get through the pain to feel the GOOD.

PREFACE

This is just the beginning!

Salty

So Salty

It fell so fast. I tried to hold it in. I thought of
every good thing that could come to mind.
Slowly, my heart sped up. My hands became
sweaty. I felt like I had no control. Do I have
control?
Am I in control?
Don't fall. Go away. But damn it, I can't see. I
need to wipe it away.
With one finger swipe to my left eye, it was like
my right eye called revenge.
You can't get rid of me that easily. That's what it
felt like it was saying.
You can't get rid of the hurt by telling me to
leave.
You cant get rid of the pain by pushing me to the
side.
You can't get rid of the embarrassment by
patting me with a tissue.
Its like the tear was telling me all this and yet I
pushed once more.
More tissues, more silent gasps for air as my
heart felt the flutter.
Not that good flutter.

Not that flutter that you feel when he touches
your hand for the first time and every time after.
Not that flutter that you feel when you feel like
you have all his attention and his heart is all
yours.
Not that flutter that you feel when that hope
sparkles inside and you say wow, he does love
me.
Not that flutter you feel when he plans all the
dates and all the trips that makes you feel like a
princess.
No!
Its that bad flutter.
That flutter that makes
That makes you studder when you talk.
That flutter that makes you tell yourself to make
those tears stop.
That flutter that tells you to push the pain to the
side and smile.
That flutter that tells you to pat those tears with
a tissue and keep it moving.
That flutter that ignores your inside cries for it is
ok.
My hands are sweaty
And damn it, these tears are so salty.

Hey You!

Hey you
I know its not nice to stare but I can't help
myself
She walked pass so I circled back and peaked
around the corner.
I wont stare, I promise I won't.
My peak turned into a look of wonder,
amazement, curiosity.
Gosh she is so striking.
How could you not take a second look.
She smiled at me and waved.
Who does that now a days?
She didn't give me a big smile.
A soft, sincere smile but a held back one. At
second glance, I saw her overbite. The soft
crookedness in her teeth that I wish I could tell
her was so beautiful and I wish she could walk
pass one more time and give me a full smile.
Her wave so graceful that I wanted her to do it
again. I saw the hairs on her arm that some
people say is disgusting and its not lady like but
it was her and her naturalness and I just wishes
she'd wave a bit slower to me.
My peak into her brown skinned face of
perfection. Not society's airbrushed perfection.

The perfection of an African American women with 3 scars of the left side that I just want to lay against my fingers and tell her I see her strength. The acne scars on the right that she didn't bother to hide today with makeup. The glow in her face that those would call oily skin and the pores that show she is living and her skin is alive just as well as she is.

I turn away. I want to know behind her eyes. Not her contacts or fancy glasses she has sitting in her hair. I want to know her behind the perfectly placed lashes. I want to know her behind the flowing hair that is so perfectly done but not too perfect placed in a bun that makes it even sexier. I want to know her voice. What the happiness sounds like. What the eagerness sounds like. What the hurt sounds like so I can make sure she never feels it again from me. I want to know her real voice. Her inner voice. Not the soft smile she hands to the world. Not the ease of letting people have their way like the gentleman who held the door for her when she'd rather go through the spinning door because it brings out the child in her heart.

One last look. I just need one more today. Let me do this one right.

I grabbed Windex. Sprayed that mirror and took one more look around that corner and into the mirror.
Hey you Eshia

3 miles in 30 minutes

3 miles in 30 minutes

I'll be there I promise.
Come on, come on, I'm making my way.
I accidentally missed my turn and now I'm non
stop down a one way.

The sounds of the car horns and the sirens meet
my ears
And what do you know, now I'm down on
Lower Wacker, my worst fears

The curves of this street, the ignoring of the
speed limit
Always tried to avoid this and I must say, I like
it.

Back to where I need to be on Lake Shore Drive
going that way
As I see the bike riders and the runners and
watch the sun set as night pushes the day
Having not been here in so long, I got so turned
around.
Even the GPS couldn't save me from looking
like a clown.

But this is my city, whether I want to deny it or
not
Come here and see Chicago and all the beauty
that it's got
From the colorful views of LondonHouse to the
fireworks at Navy Pier
This city will have something for everyone, I
promise you, just come here!

GPS says Ill be there in 30 minutes and yes I
know it's just 3 miles
Stick around and call this place home, you never
know, you may run into Simone Biles!
I'll tell you a sighting I had while having brunch
at Brass Tack in the booth right in front of me
It was DL Hughley about to enjoy a meal and
I'm like go say hi, how shy can you be?

Come to Chicago, you'll love it, you'll see
The news makes it seem like we're all monsters,
but we only softly bite, gee!

He

He's impulsive, the reaching out to women meant nothing.
He's not a liar, he just wasn't up front.
He doesn't hide things, you just didn't find it.
He's not keeping his phone face down for things to go unseen, he's keeping it face down to give you undivided attention.
He didn't mean to send you those cold messages, he's just busy.
He didn't mean to embarrass you, he's just thought you'd never know……………..
He didn't mean that he wants something serious, BUT you are his girl and he wants to see your grandma again.
He didn't mean to tell you that he wants to be best friends, BUT ask him anything except this and not that.
He didn't mean to say he doesn't want to meet you kids because then he says he thought you didn't want to introduce them.
He didn't mean to say he's crazy about you because he has been texting someone paragraphs for months when you can barely get a full sentence.

He didn't mean it when he said from now on, I
am going to tell you that I love you everyday
and make you feel special everyday because
here I am just waiting to be texted back
Goodmorning Baby.
He's not. He didn't. He never meant it. He
won't.
And Yet, he's mine?

Not A Barbie Girl In A Barbie World

She walked pass and smelled so
good;meanwhile I take a wiff to make sure my
Dove isn't wearing off after 3 hours. Or did I
wear Secret today?
She checked her lipstick after dinner; her face
perfectly matte and I can see her lipstick hasn't
budged; meanwhile my non smudge lipstick I
can barely see and my 24 hour matte makeup is
shining like a mirror.
She strolled along hand in hand in those
beautiful stilettos; meanwhile I am in flats
because after 30 minutes walking on a heel, my
feet screamed no!
She had her friend take a photo, took the phone
and said "Perfect, I love it!" ; meanwhile I have
to take 20 before I get that one that I feel is good
enough, not nearly perfect.
She took a dress to the dressing room, her legs
flawless and hairless; meanwhile here I am in
my dress exposing scars from my childhood,
varicose veins from pregnancies, and prickles of
hair raising up. Tho gosh, didn't I just shave two
days ago?

I remember having Barbies as a girl. Hairstyle
always perfectly put no matter where I tossed
them. Smiles perfect, never moved. Perfect fitted
outfit in their lovely box with the clear screening
so that you can see them clearly displayed.
Well well well
Hello world
Here I am
I am not a Barbie Girl in This Barbie World!

My Set Of Keys

I am not where I want to be. This home is not my home. These four sets of keys do not open places that belong to me.

This Gold key that I've gotten two copies of so far, this key opens a tri level house. A house that my mail goes to and where I lay my head mostly. Me laying my head here went from a couple of weeks to a few months, to now the one year anniversary of me using that key. The room in this home that is used for a storage has become a haven for two, sometimes five. This home is not my home.

These keys that look too small to fit in anything, they open doors to this gated community. All you need is the correct code to the keypad and you enter a space with so many other spaces. They even have a security system, cameras all around. We call this storage. I once had two on the East Coast which then accumulated to one more in the Midwest as well. I use my key to bring things in and over time, I begin to forget of what I actually have. I thought I would just have one storage for a few weeks. That time went to months and soon, it'll be a year and though there are walls and a roof, this keys do not open the doors to my home.

The third set of keys I have, I don't even need to insert it for it to work. I just keep it close and the doors unlock. These doors close and can pretty much take me anywhere. These doors closed even with a roof over my head will never make a home.

The fourth set of keys with a fob opens the doors to his home. Here I have a drawer. I have space in one of the medicine cabinets. I can come here when it's convenient for us both. The bed is shared with me and in these walls and this roof, I feel safe. This is not my home. These keys may or may not always be mine.

I am not where I want to be.

These keys do not open doors to my home yet.

One day.

I've Been Here Before

Seeing the empty seat across from me while hearing the voices and joyous laughter of those around me. Staring at the foam slowly fall in my cold beer.

I breathe in and breathe out.

Looking out the floor to ceiling windows, the look of the blue that feels so serene. Not as blue as Crater Lake but wow what a clear sky and a lovely day. From the 27th floor, it's as if I can see miles ahead; like my eyes are binoculars seeing on and on.

I breathe in and I breathe out.

I hadn't done this in so long. Can I call this a blind date? 34 years in this body and yet, I still wonder who I am. My solo blind date.

I breathe in and I breathe out.

I parked my car, quick to snap a photo in the garage so that I'm not okay hide and go seek in the garage. I walk myself in, sitting where I want, ordering what I want, sitting in my own silence. Enjoying my own silence. No talks of today if I don't want. No talks of the future if I don't want. No replaying the past if I don't want. No listening to gossip or the opinions of other people's lives if I don't want.

I breathe in and I breathe out.
My two favorite dishes on a plate. I enjoy my
meal, bite by bite. Taking my time. No needing
to cover my mouth for sake of conversation. No
need to entertain small talk.
I breathe in and I breathe out.
I've been here before. Hand in hand in the Willis
Tower, a time or two. Those times, I didn't
drive. I paid no attention to the parking space,
the doors were opened for me, I paid no
attention which halls to walk, I just followed. I
thought before I considered a seat, I thought
before I spoke. I ate and talked and I did not get
immersed in my own. I wanted to be exciting, I
wanted to be enjoyable company, I tried to be. In
my own, there's no trying. I just AM.
Here and now on the 67th floor of the Willis
Tower, I am immersed in me!
And I breathe in and I slowly breathe out.

Shame on me for letting you

I'm not one of your car loans, don't run me
through tons of banks until you get the terms
that work for you.
I'm not one of your rough drafts that you get to
ball up over and over and throw on the floor
until you get it right.
I'm not one of your bank accounts where you to
get to transfer and make withdrawals until there
is no more and close me because you've found a
better bank.
I'm not one of your wine tastings where you get
to take as small of a sip as you want and pour
the rest out to go on to the next one.
I'm not one of your door mats at your door step
that you get to walk on and stuff in the closet for
another that's better for the next season.
But I let you let me be an option.
Shame on me.

Loud Thoughts

For the first time in so long, I can hear myself
think.
I can hear those thoughts ringing my ears like
I'm hugging a fire alarm. I raise my hands to
cover my ears and hold as tight as I can.
The thoughts still so loud that they make my
teeth clinch. They make me close my eyes so
that I can try to take myself anywhere but here.
Anywhere but here in my loud ugly thoughts.

These horrifying thoughts of me never finding
my purpose.
These haunting thoughts of all the crazy
decisions I've made telling me I'll never make
better ones.
These terrifying thoughts of me never marrying,
ending up alone.
These awful thoughts of when my health as I
know it no longer exists.
These dreadful thoughts of if I'm parenting a
correctly or if I'm going down the right career
path, or if I'm any closer to being a better me....
Or am I just dangerously going 90 down a one
way toward the dead end sign?
I open my eyes.

I remind myself that today, today I did my best.
Yesterday is gone. Tomorrow is not yet here. In
my today, I acted according to what I thought
was best. My energy went to what I thought was
right. My presence went to where I felt it was
needed.
Today I did good.

Welcome Welcome! Come On In!

Welcome Welcome! Come On In!
Welcome To This 34 Year Old's Den.

Where there's sunshine and rainbows all around
And if it were up to me, no one would frown.
We would welcome each day anew with faith
and love
And when someone is feeling behind, I'd give
them a gentle shove.
We would have ample food to eat and teachers
for those who can't cook
Where people could leave the house without
makeup and fancy clothes, no worries of getting
a dirty second look.
Where love only grows and doesn't simply fade
away
As we grow and learn with one another with
each passing day.
Where a disagreement doesn't turn into a fight
And an opening mind is accepted with delight.
Floor to ceiling windows with no curtains or
drapes blocking the light
With the possibilities of life and the beauties of
the world always in plain sight.

Welcome Welcome Come On In!
Here we borrow and we also lend
We don't make fun or look down on those near
us.
We don't make a big deal of obstacles or put up a
fuss.
We talk them through piece by piece because I
know from experience that there can be peace.
So fall down if you must, don't rush to get up
again.
I'll sit right beside you, and when you're ready
just grab my hand.
Welcome To This 34 Year Old's Den.

With You, Can I?

Sometimes I feel like those bags that are laying outside of the donation boxes in the cold rainy weather because the box was full and now those bags are getting drenched in the rain and will smell when the sun comes out because they simply couldn't fit.

Sometimes I feel like that box of teas on a grocery store shelf in a row full of teas. My rows are still stocked, not one single box off the shelf, meanwhile other teas are all gone as people search frantically for just one more box.

Sometimes I feel like that last wire hanger in the closet. I'm all the way in the back, next to the velvet hangers, the plastic hangers, the new space efficient hangers. When I'm put to use, I'll more than likely be bent and stretched for a different purpose. I'll never feel a cashmere sweater lay upon me.

Sometimes I feel like that car in the junk yard. I've been scrapped for parts and crushed in more ways than one. You don't even know what I was before this flat piece of metal that now sits before you. Once upon a time, I was brand new and wanted by many. I was promoted and was long awaited for my release.

Can I share my feelings with you without you
labeling me as depressed?
Can I share my feelings with you without you
feeling like I'm inches from breaking?
Can I share my feelings with you and I let you in
and let you see the not so pretty?
With you, baby can I?

I Have Questions

What do you say about me taking you on a
Date?
Me opening every door for you, flowers every
time because it's the least I can do to show you
the beauty that you bring to me.
What do you say about me texting you good
morning and goodnight?
You're not gonna list of those I text, it's just you,
I'll call you to know about your day. Tell me all
the details, your highs, your lows, let your new
ideas be mine as I bring them to life for you.
What do you say about us going steady?
We make plans. We have deeper conventions.
You can let your wig down if you want, I'll wash
your hair for you. You can tell me your worries
and anxieties, I promise I'll never use them
against you.
I'll lay with you as we brainstorm and figure
ways to make them better. I'll meet your friends
and family and there will be no delay in you
meeting mine because you have my heart. Let's
life one another spiritually, mentally, physically.
In a world where so many judge, when we're
out, picture it just being you and me and I
promise there's no one who shines like you.

What do you say about walking down the aisle
with me?
We can have a wedding as big or small as you'd
like. My phone welcome for you to use and
know my password, no secrets. Know me, my
feelings, my inside world. You want to make a
mini me? My body is yours, let's show what our
love can do and bring into this world. I want to
laugh, cry, grow, learn, and spend my life
intertwined in you. Be clingy with me. Tell me
you love me every night. Call me like you would
your best friend to tell me that thing that
happened at work. Hold my hand whenever we
are out. Be as touchy as you want, I'm yours and
love is a gift every single day and I adore your
gift. Fill my camera role with selfies of us and
you.
But first, oh first will you do me the honor of
letting me take you on a date?

Daily

Start over
Change that plan
Erase and re evaluate
Change your hair
Choose a new hobby
Block those numbers
Delete those photos
Reinforce those boundaries
Get a new favorite song
Dress to your mood if you want
Book that day away if you need
Silence those notifications all you want
Cancel those plans
Discard those old mementos
Whatever makes you feel happy, find yourself
daily over and over again.

Would you?

If you were shown a movie clip of all the hurts that you would feel over your lifetime, would you choose to press play and give that life a go? Seeing yourself feel like you'll never love again after your first heart break.
The pain of you and your best friend growing into strangers.
The pain of the absence of your parents from your school events and important days of your life.
The pain of losing family, losing your brother, your sister.
The pain of losing your parents who when you were born, felt like they'd always be around.
Would you press play on the moment where you're filing for divorce?
Would you press play on that moment when your child is being bars and you wonder where you failed?
The pain of a broken home.
The pain of that eviction notice and you don't know where to turn.
The pain of medical bills piled up and you still aren't cured.

The pain of having to leave that job you love
because it just doesn't pay the bills anymore.
The pain of knowing shameful family secrets.
The pain of losing that business.
The pain of that car accident where the other
driver didn't have insurance.
The pain of breaking that bone.
The pain of being used and abused.
The pain in your head that leaves you carrying
pain meds.
Think back to all the bad times, the hard times,
the moments that felt impossible and remember
to continue.
Press play!

Alopecia

I rarely show my hair, not the hair I bought.
Not the hair that I've spent thousands on over the
years. Not the hair that I have to check the lace
on, scratch my head over, check for weird
smells.
No, not that hair.
I rarely show my hair.
The different textures that it has.
The receding and thinning front.
The patches in the back.
The shedding that seems it never ends.
The washing of it makes me feel like I have
made a wig on my own in the shower.
People say "If I had your hair, I would wear it
anyways"
People say "I wouldn't care what anyone says
about that little patch"

They don't know the feeling of having to style
your hair so that spots don't show.
They don't know the feeling of hoping the wind
doesn't blow to show what you're trying to hide.
Since 14, I've worn wigs. Every type of hair
extension that you can think of, I've had. People

judge and they say, you don't love yourself. Just
be natural. You shouldn't wear all that weave.
While I appreciate your concern, you just don't
know.
I rarely show my hair, not my real hair at least.

Hug

If I could, I'd hug the lonely out of myself.
If I could, I'd hug the ugly out of myself.
If I could, I'd hug the insecurity out of myself.
If I could, I'd hug the confusion out of myself.
If I could, I'd hug the heart pain out of myself.
Today, I can feel full of presence sitting in my
own warmth.
Today, I can look in the mirror and do my hair
and take care of my body and love what I see.
Today, I can remind myself that I am
wonderfully made and there is nothing wrong
with who I am.
Today, I can feel okay with being uncertain and
trust myself in my steps.
Today, I will tell my heart that I didn't lose out,
they lost out and I am better off.
Today, I took the morning off to have a coffee
and hug myself.

I'm that girl

I'll random to text you I love you even if I know
you know.
I'll mail you a card even though who goes to the
post office anymore.
I'll send you flowers even though it's supposed
to just be a girls thing right?
I'll do all the corny things that I'd want someone
to do for me.
I'm that girl!

I hope

I hope you enjoyed the words in this book.
I hope maybe one day, you'll take another look.
Thanks for allowing me to bring you into my world.
As you can see, it's a bit of a swirl.
It's ugly, it's beautiful, it's messy, it's me.
Thank you for coming along with on this journey!